The Debt Dietician's
BLUEPRINT for
FINANCIAL FITNESS

Joseph Anthony Aufiero III

ISBN: 978-1-6847-1555-8 (sc)
ISBN: 978-1-6847-1556-5 (e)

Library of Congress Control Number: 2019920183

Lulu Publishing Services rev. date: 06/01/2022

CONTENTS

INTRODUCTION

The great Eastern philosopher Lao Tzu once said, "The journey of a thousand miles begins with a single step." One thing that makes this quote so memorable is that it applies to nearly every aspect of our lives. Anything that is worth pursuing is going to require a considerable amount of time and effort. Whether we are trying to improve our personal fitness or increase our financial fitness, we need to establish goals and actively pursue them.

Whether it be payments on a house, car, or credit cards, for many Americans the most expensive thing being paid for is debt. While debt is something that can certainly have its uses, it is important to realize that debt is a *means* to an *end*—rather than the end itself. Debt may serve as a shortcut in the long journey to financial freedom, and while shortcuts can have their occasional uses, it is certainly a strategy that needs to be approached with caution.

Over time, most people will find themselves holding significantly more debt than they can reasonably justify. As debt grows, compounds, and consumes, the burden you are carrying will become significantly heavier. At some point, you will need to realize the truth—you've allowed your "financial figure" to get out of shape, and the debts you are carrying have serious consequences.

Having an excessive amount of debt can leave you feeling hopeless. People across the United States—and elsewhere around the world—find themselves constantly working simply to pay off their rapidly accruing interest. *Saving* becomes not only an afterthought but something that is deemed seemingly impossible. However, while you may find yourself trapped and struggling to get by, there is one important thing for you to realize: *it doesn't have to be this way forever.*

There is hope that things can improve.

The goal of this book is to create a program for you to increase your financial fitness and help you lose the financial fat. By making your financial health a priority, you can live a more efficient lifestyle and gradually transition from accumulating debt to accumulating wealth. Just as you would expect from a diet or exercise book, the change you are looking for isn't going to come overnight. Rather, our goal is to give you the tools, knowledge, and programs you need to *eventually* reach a state of financial stability.

For years, or even decades, people go through life without a financial program on how to use debt, manage debt, eliminate debt, and lastly, begin to build wealth after emerging from the seeming abyss of that never-ending cycle of working to pay debt.

The lack of initiating a program ends up costing the consumer tens of thousands or even a couple of hundred thousand dollars over the span of a few decades. Chances are that if you're reading this book, you work for your money. I can't think of why any logical reader would voluntarily pay even two, or up to twenty-five, years of their working life toward interest on debt. However, for so many, that's just the case. Whether it be paying credit cards for twenty-five years or more or a thirty-year mortgage, or swapping out a financed car every three years, money is coming out of someone's wallet and interest is being paid on debt, contributing to massive profits for the lenders.

Following this introduction, this book will contain six chapters:

1. Budgeting
2. To Rent or To Own?
3. Credit Cards
4. Buying a Car

In order to create a healthy, livable financial situation, you will need to carefully balance multiple financial objectives at once. Your car, your home, and your credit cards do not exist in a vacuum. Your finances are their own sort of cohesive organism, living, breathing, and consuming as a solitary unit.

Each of these chapters will help provide you with a blueprint for living a financially viable lifestyle. There are some things in life that are rightfully considered necessities. You need to have food on the table. You need to have a roof over your head. You need to take care of your body; this can include anything, ranging from trimming the fat to developing a sustained exercise routine. But even with these necessities—nutrition, shelter, fitness, and health—there are still quite a few changes to make that will enable you to become more financially stable.

- What does a reasonable mortgage look like?
- How can I improve my credit score? Why do I want to improve my credit score?
- Which monthly expenses can be easily reduced?
- How can my current debts be reconciled and eliminated?
- Which financial solutions will make the most sense for me and my family?
- What do I actually *need* in order to live the good life?

These are important questions many people find themselves asking along the road to financial freedom. While there may not be any easy answers, there are certainly a few tested principles that can get you moving in the right direction. Frugality, discipline, and attention to detail are just a few of the principles that will eventually turn your life around. The shackles of debt need not remain for your entire life. This all begins with you recognizing the need for financial tranquility and committing yourself to making some much-needed changes.

My goal for you is to use this book as a guide to develop a financial fitness program that will minimize the negative impact of your debt so that you can begin to build a healthier financial lifestyle. Assuming that you need to remain in debt for your entire life is a grave mistake you can easily avoid. Though there may be many challenging steps left along this long journey toward financial fitness, you have already taken the steps to come this far, so there is nothing stopping you from taking the next step forward.

CHAPTER 1

Budgeting: A Training Program for Success

If you have made an active decision to get your finances in order, congratulations. You have already taken the first of many important steps to create a tangible change and dramatically improve your life.

Nevertheless, if you are hoping to arrive to any distant location, such as a world where you are no longer burdened by debt, it will be very helpful if you have a tangible road map in your hand. Just as you wouldn't begin a workout routine without first doing some research—or even meeting with a personal trainer—you also shouldn't begin the pursuit of financial fitness without well-supported financial advice. The world of debt is often overwhelming and can easily swallow you whole. Without a clear, visible understanding of where you stand in the world of personal finance, you will be wandering aimlessly.

Many people know that budgeting is a key component of the financial planning process, yet very few people want to take the time to actually create a detailed, useful budget. They may have a rough idea of what their monthly rent or mortgage payment might be, and maybe they have a ballpark estimate for the amount they spend on groceries each week. But other than these rough and barely helpful details, numerous individuals are going through their financial journey in the dark.

Budgeting involves much more than checking your bank account once a month and making ballpark estimates of what your current expenses might be.

Why are so few people willing to put in the time and effort to create a workable budget?

Maybe it is because they do not have the time. Maybe it is because they are not sure how a budget is actually made. But often people choose not to make a budget because they do not want to face the reality of their current financial situation. The constant sense of denial felt by people with excessive debt is not unlike the sense of denial felt by people facing major health issues. Though you may not want to, it's time for you to brace yourself and step on the financial scale, even if you don't like the figure that appears. At least you'll be aware of where the starting line is.

The denial of one's financial status is a widespread problem that needs to be addressed. This is how credit card companies and other lenders are able to get away with financial murder. They know that they can charge whatever they legally can, and due to a lack of knowledge and even out of sheer desperation, many people will blindly pay.

While the phrase "Work smarter, not harder" may be cliché, it certainly presents a lot of hidden wisdom. You could continue in your current state of financial panic; clipping coupons in the newspaper is certainly a wise and frugal thing to do. Unfortunately, this is a *reactive* response to an already unstable financial situation. Instead of being reactive, you can make an even bigger difference by being *proactive.* Looking at the numbers on paper and in front of you will help you identify unnecessary expenses you never even realized you had. The truth is *in the numbers.* Making an intelligent decision to work smarter instead of simply working harder can create the change you are hoping for.

The first phase of financial fitness is to evaluate your situation and try to think about your typical day. Not having a budget is like going to the gym to lose weight without having a training program. A little of this and a little of that is ineffective for losing weight. A weight-loss program is paramount to achieve success, just as a financial budget program is to obtain real financial fitness. For maximum efficiency and precision, try to follow a budget. Each month try to perform this budget as you earn and spend money.

There are a few basic principles that can help all budgeters achieve their goals:

- Accurately record all expenses, even if you don't like what you're writing down.
- Be realistic with your expectations. Prioritize your expenses so you can easily determine what you can afford and what is beyond your reach.
- Credit should be viewed as a *backup plan* rather than a simple default.
- Be willing to make changes over time.

While these principles are just the tip of the iceberg, they can help you orient yourself and begin establishing budgeting practices that can be sustained over time.

Below you will see a budget template. Budgeting is similar to calorie counting when you're trying to lose weight. Dieters who observe and scrutinize their calorie intake during the day often have much better results than people who eat with no game plan. The same holds true for financial fitness. What you will find is that, over time, your success rate will improve as you improve with budgeting. Many people suffer from "death by a thousand cuts," but as your experience grows, your cash flow will improve, and you will increase your financial fitness!

Month:	

Income	
Source 1	
Source 2	

Source 3	
Source 4	
Total:	

Expenses	
Auto Gas	
Auto Insurance	
Bank Loans	
Beer/Wine	
Cable/Dish	
Cell Phones	
Charity	
Childcare	
Cigarettes	
Clothes	
Condo Fees	
Dental Insurance	
Dining Out	
Dry Cleaning	
Electricity	
Entertainment	
Groceries	
Haircuts/Hair Care	
Health Insurance	
Housekeeping	
Internet	
Landline Telephone	
Laundry	
Lawn Care	
Lunch Money	
Medical Copays	
Medication	

Memberships	
Mortgage	
Motorcycle	
Natural Gas	
Office Supplies	
Pet Care	
Property Taxes	
Religious Giving	
School Supplies	
Security Services	
Sewer	
Student Loans	
Subscriptions	
Trash	
Union Dues	
Vehicle Payment	
Vehicle Payment 2	
Water Bill	
Total:	

Income	
Expenses	
Cash flow	

As you can see, there are many things that will need to be considered when calculating your monthly budget. However, by dividing your budget into different components, you can identify areas where you can potentially cut back on costs. Keeping track of your monthly spending and earnings as they fluctuate month to month will also make it easier to make the right financial decisions.

If you are feeling a bit of a sting from creating your first official budget, you are certainly not alone. In fact, you might feel similar to an athlete who just experienced the first of many grueling workouts. After multiplying each of these figures by 12, for example, you are probably realizing just how much you are spending per year on certain things.

For instance, if you smoke a pack of cigarettes per day, which costs on average $6.16 in the United States, this means you are spending $2,248.40 *per year* on cigarettes. Even a two-dollar cup of coffee every day will run you more than seven hundred dollars annually. If you spend fifty dollars per week going out to dinner or getting drinks with friends, that is another twenty-six hundred dollars you are spending each year.

Now it will be up to you to decide what to do and how you spend your money. However, regardless of what you choose, it will be crucial to pay close attention to *what you are actually spending.* The hundreds—even thousands—of small purchases made throughout the year will combine to produce the aforementioned death by a thousand cuts. For example, if someone slashed three small expenses (e.g., cigarettes, going out, and paying for coffee), he or she would immediately save more than five thousand dollars per year. Depending on where you live, that may be enough to pay rent for six months.

Since we can all agree a penny saved is a penny earned, what would you be willing to do for a five-thousand-dollar raise?

The Purpose of Creating a Budget
Now you are probably thinking, *Do they really expect me to never go out for coffee or a beer ever again?*

The answer to this question is obviously no. In this journey of a thousand miles, it is important to realize there are many possible steps right in front of you. Most of these steps will require you to make some small changes to your lifestyle choices.

Is taking the stairs instead of the elevator a minor inconvenience? Yes, but when repeated regularly over time, this action will have a positive impact on your overall fitness.

Is making coffee at home instead of going to Starbucks a minor inconvenience? Yes, but when you think of the hundreds of dollars you can save each year, you'd probably be much more willing to make a change. Even if you could make an *incremental* change—cutting your coffee runs from five times a week to three times a week—this will have a major impact on your long-term financial well-being.

Instead of trying to find the magic switch that will eliminate your debt and provide you with a state of financial stability in one fell swoop, you'd be much better off looking for the many tiny steps that can carry you along your epic journey. For example, if you could find just ten ways to save twenty dollars per month, you will have already cut out twenty-four hundred dollars in yearly expenses. This is the financial equivalent of reducing your rent or monthly mortgage payments by two hundred dollars.

The purpose of creating a budget is to make it as easy as possible to identify potential savings opportunities. Before creating your first budget, it might be helpful for you to guesstimate the appropriate amount of spending each month. Then, once you can compare your ideal numbers against the actual numbers, it will be easier to see where these potential savings opportunities exist.

Suppose that, based on your understanding of your current financial situation, you believe that you can reasonably spend two hundred dollars per month going out with your friends. When you go through your bank statements and conclude that you spent $450 per month, on average, over the past few months, you will be shocked. After all, this means you are functionally spending three thousand dollars more per year than you deemed to be appropriate (out of fifty-four hundred dollars total).

Most people budget on a monthly basis, but depending on your current situation, you may want to create a budget that is shorter or longer. Regardless, the entire budgeting process should remain with clear *before, during,* and *after* components.

1. *Before the month begins:* Estimate your total income from the month and add up all of your predetermined expenses (insurance, mortgage, car payment, and so on). This will make it easy for you to recognize the level of discretionary income you currently have to work with.

2. *During the month:* Create a spreadsheet or use your favorite budgeting software. Enter all expenses (preferably categorized) and incomes as they occur throughout the course of the month. If it is only midway through the month and you have already spent 75 percent of the funds you allocated toward food, then you may need to make some necessary spontaneous adjustments.

3. *At the end of the month:* Compare your actual expenses and incomes to the figures you initially projected. Were you spending more than you should be? Were you surprisingly frugal? Keeping these figures, as well as your long-term financial objectives, in mind will help you move into the next month with ease.

When creating a budget, it is very important that you are completely honest with yourself. Many people with habits considered vices—such as smoking, excessive eating, excessive shopping, drinking, and so on—have problems accepting how much they are actually spending. However, if you are unable to be honest with yourself, you will never be able to achieve your long-term financial objectives. The first step to fixing any wound—financial or otherwise—is recognizing where the bleeding originated. Only then can you begin to stitch things back up.

Developing Clear Financial Goals

One of the most important things to do when creating a budget is to develop a clear set of financial objectives. After all, knowing whether your ship is on course is only possible when you know where the final destination might be.

When developing a list of goals, you should try to include both short-term and long-term objectives. This will help you create a budget that can help you actually achieve what you've set out to accomplish.

Some common financial objectives include the following:

- saving a specific amount of money each month (if you are making fifty thousand dollars per year, consider trying to save one thousand dollars per month)
- Being able to afford a larger house, a nicer car, or make another major purchase
- Sending your kids to college
- Being able to retire at a reasonable age
- Advancing your career—this may include getting the money to go back to school, start your own business, or take another major financial risk
- Living a life that is both comfortable and debt-free

When your goals are decades long-term, it can be difficult to commit yourself to pursuing them. If you currently have large amounts of debt eating into your limited surplus pay, pursuing these objectives can be even more difficult. For instance, if you are twenty-five and plan on retiring at sixty-five, saying goodbye to your hard-earned money for forty years isn't something you want to do. Nevertheless, the earlier you commit yourself to pursuing a specific objective, the easier it will be for you to actually achieve it.

Instead of simply striving to "improve my finances" as a goal, it will be much more beneficial for you to create smaller goals you can actually use. One of the most popular methods for creating reasonable goals—both among businesses and ambitious individuals—is known as the "SMART" goal system.

SMART goals have five defining characteristics. They are:

- *Specific:* Defining exactly what you hope to achieve will make achieving it significantly easier.
- *Measurable:* Having a clear, quantitative definition of your objectives will help you determine whether or not you were successful.

- *Achievable:* In order for a goal to be useful, it should simultaneously motivate you to change while still being reasonably within reach.
- *Relevant:* The goal needs to be directly tied to your financial well-being.
- *Time bound:* By having a realistic time frame for when you expect to achieve your goals, you will be motivated to change the status quo.

This system of creating goals can be applied to almost every aspect of life. Once you know the person you desire to be in the future, it will be much easier for you to make the necessary changes.

Your goals are not something you should simply write down on paper and then forget about. This, among other reasons, is why so few people are actually able to follow through with their New Year's resolutions. Instead, your goals should be revisited and reevaluated on a regular basis. When reviewing your goals—both financial and otherwise—try to examine what has changed, what you've been doing well, and ways that you can improve. Though perfection remains beyond our mortal reach, making progress is still very possible.

"Active" Budgeting

In a way, your budget is a sort of quantitative method for capturing your financial goals. Just as the pursuit of any goal requires an active, hands-on approach, developing an active approach to budgeting will be absolutely crucial.

Creating a budget alone will not be enough for you to suddenly become financially stable. The purpose of creating a budget, like weighing yourself or clocking your mile time, is for you to get a better understanding of where you are in the status quo and which changes need to be made. It will be entirely up to you to bridge the gap between your financial ideal and your financial reality. With every transaction you make, you should be thinking about whether it is or is not compatible with your already existing budget. If it's not compatible, ask yourself, *Why am I making this purchase?*

Is the budget the problem? Or is your inability to stick with your financial goals the problem? At the end of the day, you likely know which answer is actually right.

When creating an active budget, you will need to begin to discover your potential sources of financial bleeding. Marking each item within your budget with an "N" or a "U" can help you easily distinguish which costs are *necessary* and which costs are *unnecessary*. Some people prefer to use a 1 to 5 scale (1 being not at all necessary and 5 being absolutely necessary) in order to add a bit more depth to their budget analysis.

However, even within the category of items that are deemed "Necessary," such as food or rent, there will still be many ways that you can potentially clot the bleeding. For example, while food may be necessary, going out to dinner four nights a week is something you can easily cut back on. While shelter may be necessary, it will not be worthwhile to burden yourself with a mortgage you cannot afford. Essentially, every category within your budget likely represents a way you can *stop the bleeding* to a certain degree. It will be up to you to pay close attention to the details.

The financial bleeding often stems from many sources. Imagine each morning:

- What is it that you do when you wake up in the morning?
- What are the things that you do during the course of a typical day that cost you money?
- Are there any specific things that you can do to reduce or eliminate daily habits that cost you money?

For some people it might be a morning coffee at their community's new and trendy coffee shop. For other people it might be a long shower. Others might have steak with their eggs; as you might already know, too much red meat is expensive and has been linked to age-related diseases.

Still others might turn on the television. You know, I'm still amazed how many consumers are paying over two hundred dollars per month for cable television. That's over twenty-four hundred dollars per year, and about equal to one month's take-home income for so many of our readers. Again, what would you be willing to do in order to get a raise of this size?

Imagine getting up in the morning, taking a shower, brushing your teeth, making a quick breakfast, fighting traffic to get to work, and dealing with your boss and the stress of your job. Then, of course, the whole process of getting you home— yes, doing all that for a whole month just to provide your household with cable television!

Here are some common tips for cutting back on your living expenses. They may fatten your wallet and reduce your waistline too!

- Downsize your home. The savings can be huge with a lower mortgage, lower property taxes, and even lower utility bills.
- Avoid the use of credit cards when possible; they're almost always expensive.
- Turn off the lights when possible.
- Upgrade from incandescent light bulbs to fluorescent. Here the savings give twice; they use less energy and last longer.
- Unplug all electrical appliances that draw a current. The appliances could be "off" but could still be drawing energy.
- During the winter, if possible, use a wood stove for home heating. Shredded paper makes great free kindling too.
- Reduce your water consumption, for example, take shorter showers.
- Hang your clothes to dry instead of using a dryer—your clothes will last longer too.
- Review your phone services; having both a landline phone and a cell phone is largely unnecessary .
- Consider a low-cost internet provider.
- Prepare your own food; typically prepackaged food is more expensive and loaded with chemicals.

- Eat less meat and try to replace it with beans.
- Add rice as a side with your meals. A fifty-pound bag of rice costs about twenty dollars online and can last in a large family's household for over a month.
- Learn to make soups. For example, carrots are a dollar per pound at the grocery store. Lentil beans can be added to increase the hardiness of the soup at the cost of about one dollar per pound. As you can see, it's possible to feed a family of five for less than five dollars a day.
- Drink filtered tap water instead of soda or bottled water.
- Cook dinner on the weekends. Dining out adds up over the course of a year!
- Use cloth towels instead of paper.
- Shoes often last for two years or more; sneakers are way more expensive over time.
- Plant a home garden. If you have a backyard with a lawn, it's inefficient. Think of all the time necessary to water the lawn and cut the grass, and the money spent on fertilizer. It's costly for so many and provides very little. Rather than grass, think fruits, vegetables, and even trees. A couple of plum trees can provide a large yield of fruit during those warm summer days. It's a great hobby, and you could grow a whole summer's worth of organic fruit and vegetables for close to free.
- Is a second car really necessary? Having only one car saves money with gas and auto insurance. Keeping your car longer also saves you money. Even if the car costs two thousand dollars in repairs per year, it's still much cheaper than your typical new-car payment. Some consumers even go further by eliminating the car altogether and replacing it with ride-sharing apps.
- If you need to make a purchase, look for used instead of new. Apps like Letgo and Decluttr offer products for often pennies on the dollar.

The facts are that if you're precise with your budgeting, you can generate savings. It's amazing what a few little changes can do over the span of many years.

To really capture the power of savings, consider that if you cut the financial fat, pulled only two hundred twenty-five dollars per month out of your budget, and contributed that each month into an investment for twenty-five years with an annual compounded interest rate of 7 percent, you would have over $183,000 dollars in savings. It's truly amazing, life changing, and something that might even echo through subsequent generations. For many people, this can be the difference between filing bankruptcy and early retirement. In further support, the financially fittest individuals, that is, millionaires and billionaires, use this method to preserve and grow their wealth. So if the best time to plant a fruit tree is twenty years ago, the second-best time is today. Evaluate your budget now!

The Bottom Line

If this is your first time reading about budgeting, you may find yourself a bit overwhelmed. However, there are quite a few takeaways that anybody—even Warren Buffett—could immediately apply to their lives.

- Only purchase things that are reasonably necessary.
- Keep careful track of all your purchases—even the ones you regret.
- Develop a habit of actively making and sticking to your budget.
- Remember the importance of discipline, frugality, and attention to detail.
- Remember that the good life often comes from things without a price tag.

Even in the face of what appears to be an endless journey, there is still a light that can guide you forward. With complete awareness of your financial situation, you can make the changes you need in order to make measurable progress. Do your future self a favor and start making these important changes today.

CHAPTER 2

To Rent or To Own?

One of our most natural instincts is to find a place we can call home.

We look around our world and see birds building nests, wolves laying claim to cozy dens, and deer finding a safe place in the woods to sleep at night. Suddenly, we realize we are not so different from animals who share our world. However, there is one thing about the human lifestyle that cannot possibly be ignored—if we want a place to comfortably lay our heads at night, we are going to have to pay for it.

In a world where resources are scarce, securing the means for adequate shelter will require us to play into the system, carefully save, and then find a home that is within our means. But while these things may all be obvious, you are likely already finding yourself running into quite a few dilemmas.

- How much home can I reasonably afford?
- When, if ever, is the right time for me to purchase a home?
- How much debt can I safely assume when taking out a mortgage?
- Should I decide to rent or to own?

As we mentioned throughout the budgeting chapter, the answers to these burning questions will be highly dependent on your current living and financial situations. For some people, renting will be the most financially justifiable option. For others, purchasing a home will have much clearer benefits.

When trying to answer these critical questions, there will be no such thing as easy answers. Instead, it will be important for you to search deeper and try to view the situation from as many different angles as you possibly can.

When searching for wisdom, I often look back to family members who shared their ideas with me, whether by example or by conversations many years ago. Chances are that you had at least one member of your family who was a financial success, be it a parent, grandparent, aunt, or uncle. When I'm about to move forward with a decision related to money, I often try to visualize in my mind how this successful financial role model would have responded given the situation.

My grandparents once lived in Boston's North End, the neighborhood of Paul Revere. This community is also known as "Little Italy," made famous by clean streets, fine dining, pastry shops, and summer feasts that continue for days. However, it's very densely populated, with large brick buildings connected in rows, thus lacking a lot of elbow room for growing families, backyards, and sufficient parking. My grandfather was very comfortable living in the area, but my grandmother wanted a garden, fruit trees, and a place for their children to run, ride their bikes, and play sports.

At the time, their living situation was financially ideal since they lived in a family-owned four-unit apartment building, each apartment stacked on top of the other. My grandfather realized that a single family house was an immediate debt liability for him; in layman's terms, it was basically something that would reliably bleed him dry each month. Having seen the benefits of multifamily living already, he decided to buy a multifamily home with the look and feel of a single family.

After some time searching, they decided on a bedroom community just outside of Boston. The cost of owning this house would be subsidized by the rental income of the second floor. Furthermore, my grandparents enjoyed favorable mortgage terms since my grandfather qualified for the GI Bill, having been a United States Army combat veteran.

While these reflections and experience may be incredibly personal, they are hardly different from what many American families have experienced themselves. While this may be the land of opportunity, it is very rarely the land of success without hard work. The United States has always been a land with a sort of magnetic property; despite being one of the last places on earth to be populated by humans, it has drawn people from walks of life from all across the world. Within this land there has always been a sort of unspoken arrangement: in exchange for freedom, it will be up to you to find a way to make ends meet.

We can debate the politics of this arrangement for hours, but it is a facet of our American reality that can simply not be ignored. In order to move up in the world, you may need to make compromises. My grandparents made compromises when they decided to live in a duplex instead of a stand-alone home. My family made compromises when they left their old world villages in order to risk it all and discover the land of opportunity. Finding an adequate living situation is not always easy, but it is something that—even by those who are most down on their luck—can eventually be achieved.

When deciding where you hope to live, the first thing you will need to ask yourself is: *What kind of compromises are you willing to make? Are you willing to make sacrifices in the status quo in order to create a more comfortable future?*

My family's original 4 unit apartment building in Boston's North End.

The Benefits of Owning a Home

Keeping the American spirit in mind, it seems there are few ambitions that are more natural in this country than the pursuit of homeownership. Homeownership is something that is a natural extension of the principles the United States was founded on—life, liberty, and the pursuit of happiness are all values that reach their zenith within the personal home. In this long trek toward financial fitness, owning a home may feel like training for a marathon: overwhelming at first, but oh so satisfying once it is actually achieved.

However, the benefits of owning a home are more than simply romanticized abstractions. In fact, the benefits of owning a home are incredibly tangible:

- The ability to actively keep a portion of your equity, rather than surrendering your rent to a property manager every month
- The pride you can have in owning, caring for, and—eventually—enhancing something that is truly your own
- Access to greater privacy and the ability to live life freely

- Predictable costs that are easier to manage (especially for anyone who has been able to secure a fixed-rate mortgage)
- Various tax benefits that can help reduce your annual tax obligations
- An asset that is (typically) appreciating in value, allowing you to accumulate equity to an even greater extent

With all of these benefits potentially within your reach, you are likely thinking about the prospects of becoming a homeowner yourself. Aspiring to become a homeowner *someday* is an ambition that is both beautiful and commendable. However, though you may be excited to be taking the next step forward, it is important to remember that home ownership is not without its fair share of costs.

The Costs of Owning a Home

The most obvious cost of owning a home is the *total interest* you will end up paying. While it will be nice to have a portion of your mortgage returned back to you each month (in the form of accumulating equity), it is also important to remember that a large portion of your mortgage is being surrendered to the bank. Though it may pain you to admit it, your mortgage is another—likely the largest—source of personal debt. Purchasing a home that you are simply incapable of affording can result in decades of financial woes.

According to the data from the Census Bureau, as of 2018 the home ownership rate in the United States is 64.8 percent. While this figure is marginally lower than it was in the past, it should give you hope that you don't need to be in the "1 percent" in order to own a home. However, of this large population of homeowners, there are still many people who have a mortgage that is simply unmanageable. We saw the aftermath of this issue in 2008 with the housing crisis. Based on current trends and human instincts, we will likely see history repeat itself with more of these boom-and-bust housing cycles in the future.

With the goal of not being a participant of the cyclical housing bust, the true *cost* of owning a home is something every discerning homeowner should be aware of before jumping in on the home of their dreams.

- Making a long-term financial commitment that can be incredibly difficult to get out of (at least without loss)
- Committing a large portion of your equity to an illiquid asset
- Potential value loss during periods of economic uncertainty
- Costs such as the initial down payment (likely 3.5–20 percent of the total purchase price), the cost of moving, and closing costs
- Regular fees such as homeowners' association fees, homeowners' insurance, and mortgage insurance (when applicable)
- Increased utility bills and the need to pay for repairs
- The risk of becoming "house poor" (a situation where you have wealth/personal equity, but all of your wealth is committed to your home)

When the benefits and drawbacks of owning a home are listed right next to one another, making your final decision can be significantly more difficult. The costs of owning a home are likely much more than you originally assumed and are almost certainly more than what a real estate agent will readily tell you. But while these costs should certainly give you reason to approach the home-buying market with a greater degree of caution, they should not deter you from pursuing your lifelong dreams altogether.

Establishing Realistic Expectations

When thinking about your housing options, it is important for you to be realistic. While the banks certainly deserve plenty of blame for the recent housing crisis of 2007–2008, there is no doubt that people purchasing homes beyond their means was one major contributing factor. As mortgages across the country simultaneously began to default, both the banking and housing industries ran into a major cash flow crisis.

If you are considering purchasing a new home, one of the most important things for you to realize is this:

Just because you qualify for a mortgage doesn't mean you can necessarily afford that mortgage.

When banks are issuing mortgages, they are still concerned with your credit score, but they are more concerned about your raw ability to pay back whatever loan they issue. These banks are in it for the long haul and will happily issue any mortgage that can lead to significant profits down the line. Even if your credit score is subpar or you have been late on a payment, or two, or three, or even more, the potential of collecting interest equal to almost the original purchase price of the home is very tempting and allows justification for their initial decision to issue the loan.

Instead of trying to see what the banks will *let* you borrow, it is much better to take a step back and try to objectively determine what you are actually *able* to borrow and afford.

The budgeting exercises completed in the first chapter should help you determine your current level of discretionary income and the amount of wiggle room you currently have in your budget. Your mortgage will represent a major source of financial fat, and it is one that should be accepted with caution. Even if you think you are able to account for every aspect of home ownership, be sure not to get too ahead of yourself. There *will* be unexpected costs down the road, and the total cost of a home *will* be greater than you initially assumed.

This is where developing realistic expectations is something that is so fundamentally important. When comparing your options, ask yourself the following things:

- How much value does a pool *really* add to a home?
- How often are people going to *really* need to use the extra guest room?
- Does having an extra bathroom *really* justify a second mortgage?
- What percentage of my paycheck am I *really* willing to give up in order to live five minutes closer to work?

If the people in these scenarios could have made even one small sacrifice, they could likely have secured a drastically different mortgage that was much more compatible with their budget. While housing itself is certainly an unavoidable necessity, living a life of luxury is exactly that—a luxury.

As one of the largest expenses on your current budget sheet, being reasonable with your living situation is one of the clearest ways for you to trim your financial fat.

An Alternative Option: Following the Footsteps of My Grandparents

I am aware that the tone of this chapter has been mostly pessimistic toward home ownership. But the deliberately stern tone has *not* been used because we are opposed to people becoming homeowners—in fact, the reality of the situation is quite the opposite. What we are opposed to is people purchasing homes beyond their means and chaining themselves to a lifetime of debt.

If you are determined to become a homeowner, there are still plenty of options that can help make this dream a reality. Again, as we saw with the Starbucks drinker who made the decision to drink their coffee at home, being willing to make just a few small sacrifices can have a tremendous impact on your long-term financial well-being.

As previously stated, with a typical home purchase, most consumers are on a payment plan that will cost them almost double the contracted purchase price. So a house that costs two hundred thousand dollars will probably cost around three hundred seventy thousand dollars over the span of thirty years, with the banks pulling in the lion's share of the difference between the price at closing and the amount actually paid. Remember, my grandparents avoided such a scenario as a result of rental income and favorable mortgage terms. They avoided paying almost double the debt amount incurred at the time of purchase and were set up for success with their first home purchase.

Below see a table of a basic comparative analysis between a single family home and a duplex that offers a "mortgage helper" apartment. For conceptual ease, insurance, rental income, and taxes have remained static throughout this analysis.

Single Family Home		Duplex Home	
Cost	$300,000.00	Cost	$330,000.00
Monthly Mortgage Payment 4.5% interest rate,·3.5% down.·Annual taxes at $2000.·Annual insurance at $1000.	$1,716.86	Monthly Mortgage Payment 4.5% interest rate,·3.5% down.·Annual taxes at $2500.·Annual insurance at $1200.	$1,921.87
Amount Paid over 30 years	**$618,069.60**	**Amount Paid over 30 years**	**$691,873.20**
		Monthly Rental Income	$1,500.00
		Rental income over 30 years	**$540,000.00**
Amount Paid out of Pocket	**$618,069.60**	**Amount Paid out of Pocket**	**$151,873.20**
	Single Family Mortgage Cost per month	$1,716.86	
	Duplex Buyer Cost per Month (Mortgage-Rental Income)	$421.87	
	Amount of Money Saved per Month	$1,294.99	
	Duplex Buyer Savings Paying This over 30 Years	**$466,196.40**	

As you can see above, the duplex homeowner actually paid back *less* than the sale price of the house due to the rental revenue. A single family home would have cost about half a million dollars more, and clearly that money could be working for their family better elsewhere. In addition, there are tax benefits to owing a duplex over a single family home. For example, many repairs or a portion of the repairs can be written off.

Below is some serious food for thought. Now imagine if the duplex homeowner invests the difference ($1,294.99) into a mutual fund with an annual rate of return at 7 percent compounded annually. Over the span of thirty years, the fund would be valued at over 1.5 million dollars. Below is a table showing the results.

If the Amount of Money Was Saved in a Mutual Fund over 30 Years with: Monthly contributions of $1294.99, Hypothetical Annual Rate of Return at 7% Compounded Annually	
Amount Contributed	$466,196.40
Investment Ending Balance	$1,522,992.10

Millions of homes are bought and sold each year. Millions of people are moving forward without analyzing the financial impact of home ownership on their budget. A home purchase is a really huge financial fork in the road, perhaps the largest that you will ever see. Its impact to you and your family will have an effect for decades. All too often it's too emotional, and people often overlook the logic. For the sake of this comparison, we could say that both home buyers have regular Joe Six-pack incomes/expenses. However, in this hypothetical situation, over the span of three decades, with just a couple of simple changes, *one has over a million dollars more than the other.*

It's my opinion that home ownership is often pumped up in the public discussion by the media. Ask yourself a couple of questions: Who might benefit from this? How might companies/individuals be benefiting from this?

Here's the truth: Banks benefit from a large number of consumers buying houses and paying interest for thirty years. Banks pay a lot of money in advertising, which allows them a large voice in mass media, such as the television, radio, and the internet. By way of political donations, they're the biggest financial backers of both political parties, and it's not by coincidence that many home purchases are actually federally insured. Those buyers who elect to buy a home with a minimum of 3.5 percent down and are not putting down 20 percent almost always fall into an FHA mortgage product. If this type of buyer stops paying, the lender has a right to file a claim for the losses with a government agency known as the Federal Housing Administration (FHA). So in a nutshell, banks and politicians have developed the "one hand washes the other" relationship, and the whole mortgage industry is supported on the back of the employed Joe Six-pack.

With every pro and con attached to each decision you can possibly make, you should ask yourself: *What is the specific cost of this?* Having a shared wall with a neighbor can be a minor annoyance. Is this annoyance one that can justify the lost opportunity of more than *half a million* dollars over the course of thirty years? Having to commute an additional ten minutes to work can also be a minor annoyance. But again, does this commute justify sinking an additional 25 percent of your income into a mortgage? What is it, specifically, that you are even working toward in the first place?

Where could that large savings be used to potentially better your life? Are you willing to shackle yourself to decades of debt for the simple sake of having a few luxuries?

Determining the Opportunity Cost of an Investment

One of the problems with many people flirting with the prospect of home ownership is that they fail to account for the *opportunity cost* of the investment they are making. Purchasing a $500,000 home doesn't "really" cost you $500,000—instead, it costs you whatever it is you would have done with that money instead.

If the difference between a $500,000 home and a $400,000 home, for example, was not just interpreted as $100,000, but instead was "translated" to mean retiring five years earlier, there would likely be many more home buyers who would reevaluate their initial decision. If you, like many people, are in the process of trying to carefully balance saving for retirement, saving for your kids to go to college, and saving to provide for everything else, the opportunity cost of a given investment will be significantly higher. By saying yes to one thing, you are consequently saying no to countless others.

As you could see in the section above, the Joe Six-pack who invested his savings to make his money work for him by buying the duplex over the single family home was wealthier as a result. Now let's imagine that Joe Six-pack never bought a house in the first place and paid one thousand dollars per month for rent. Yes, the rent is cheaper, but the saving goes further—no home repairs, homeowner insurance, or property taxes. All other things being equal, he could afford to invest $716.86 per month (the amount equal to the difference between the monthly mortgage payment and the monthly rent) into an account over thirty years. With a hypothetical annual rate of return at 7 percent compounded annually, this consumer's account would be worth $843,073.63 at the end of that thirty years.

The single family home will be worth less than the investment even though the home might be worth over four hundred thousand dollars after the span of thirty years—but it could also be worth less than that. Believe it or not, diversified mutual funds are more stable than single family housing over the span of time, and history proves just that. Don't believe me? Ask the people who bought homes in Detroit twenty-five years ago or people who purchased homes in the rust belt with only a single employer in their town that went overseas or belly-up. The value of coal country homes burned up pretty quickly as public opinion changed and government regulation increased. At best, the value of those homes went sideways.

The reality of the result mostly depends on you. Generally speaking, renters tend to spend the savings on consumer goods and do not develop superior skills for saving. Homeownership does encourage saving, because a portion of the monthly payment eventually gets converted to home equity. Although it's largely inefficient compared to investing, it's better than doing nothing at all (renting and spending).

A renter who spends is the worst case in this scenario. Their money disappears with the purchase of the latest and greatest gaming system, clothes, new sneakers, or automobile. Conversely, if a renter can implement a budget, maintain a savings plan, and reliably set money aside each month, the data show that it's a method generally superior to building wealth over the method of homeownership.

Clearly, deciding whether to rent or to own a home is a decision that can be incredibly complicated. Even within each of these decisions, there will be several important other decisions that will immediately spawn in response (for example, if you have decided to purchase a home, you will need to decide whether to purchase a duplex or a single family home). No matter what, trying to quantitatively analyze all of the options you have available can help you feel much more confident in whatever final choice you make.

Deciding whether Renting or Owning Is Right for You

Now we are finally beyond the meat and potatoes of this chapter. You've thought about your current financial situation, and you've developed a very cautious approach. At the end of the day, does it make more sense for you to rent, buy or sell your current home?

Unfortunately, there are still no easy answers to this question. Any answers you receive from a real estate agent, lender, or property manager will likely be skewed by their own selfish intentions. Talk is cheap, and this has a limited amount of usefulness. The reason why answering this question is so fundamentally difficult is that there are so many variables that are specific to you and you alone.

However, while we are not in the business of providing cheap answers, we are certainly in the business of providing sound advice.

Planning Your Next Big Move

If after these crucial words of caution, you are determined to purchase a home, it will be important for you to engage in a thorough and comprehensive process. By being able to account for as much as you can in advance, you are unlikely to run into financial surprises in the future.

It is impossible for us to know which decisions will be in your financial best interest. But there are a few guidelines that can make planning your next big move a bit more reasonable:

- Assume everything costs more than you initially think.
- Be realistic about the amount of home you can afford.
- There is a reason why the more expensive home is the one that you like more; don't get sucked in to the "open house trap."
- As we will continue to state, true happiness—or the good life—comes from something much deeper than material possessions.

Obviously you do need a place to live. Beyond this simple fact of life, it will be up to you to secure a place and live responsibly. Ask yourself, *Will the person I become thirty years from now be happy with the decisions I am making today?*

Proverbs 22:7 King James Version (KJV)
The rich ruleth over the poor, and the borrower is
servant to the lender.

CHAPTER 3

Credit Cards

Plastic ... while being nothing more than a petroleum product, it seems this specific material has changed the world seemingly more than any other. With plastic, it is now possible for manufacturers to accurately mold and create anything they can imagine. But perhaps even more importantly, plastic has indirectly enabled people to pay for things *without money in their pockets.*

Yes, we are aware that checks have been around much longer than credit cards or debit cards, but I believe you understand our underlying point. Having risen from obscurity over the course of the past century, the credit card industry has asserted itself as one of the most important components of the global economy. However, the industry itself is undeniably bittersweet: while credit makes it possible for people to buy now and pay later, it is also allows the possibility for consumers to assume a level of debt they simply cannot afford.

Managing your credit card situation will be one of the most important components of your plan to become financially fit. Credit cards are a common source of financial debt that will drag you down and leave you feeling sluggish in the future. Because credit cards have established themselves as mainstream in our society, many people assume that using these cards is standard or can generally be considered the default payment option. While it is true that most people will use a credit card at some point in their lives, believe it or not, in the United States there are currently more than 300 million Visa cards in circulation. When added along with other credit cards, there are more than two cards issued for every American adult. What is not true, however, is the idea that credit cards are an *absolute* necessity.

I recall once speaking with a prospective client who was elderly; he might have been in his mid-seventies. He told me that he was struggling with some high-interest-rate credit card debt. As it turns out, he had been charging a little here and there and paying the minimums since the 1990s. The debt he carried was basically like a bad gym membership that he wanted to terminate but couldn't. The interest he paid kept this membership open and active. At that moment in time, his debt membership was costing him about seven hundred dollars in interest per month. Who would pay almost ten thousand dollars a year for a membership that is barely used? It's cockamamie! Yet people do just that all the time. Because the amount charged, debt amounts, and monthly payment amounts varied over the years, it was impossible to tally all of the interest he paid. However, he informed me that over the years, he was carrying a collective balance with all of his credit cards to the tune of about thirty thousand dollars. As it turns out, he spent at minimum over $180,000 in interest over decades that he had been charging and paying. He still had the debt and not much to show for it.

As with home mortgages, banks also really push credit cards to help continue an endless debt cycle. By the time a person is eighteen, they have already been exposed to years of advertising by lenders to create the idea that debt is easy, necessary, and even offers financial freedom. The reality is that credit cards offer financial freedom to the lenders, which leads to consumers packing on financial fat.

When contemplating the possibility of applying for a new credit card, the first thing you should ask yourself is: *Is this really necessary?*

What would happen if you would forgo the card and continue paying for things in cash?

What would happen if you were to save and delay your next major purchase for a month—or even longer?

How much are you willing to pay to have money today, rather than waiting for your next few paychecks to come through?

For some people, applying for a credit card might be necessary. An unexpected circumstance could come up in life where credit is necessary. Fat does have certain biological uses, after all. Options such as applying for a high-interest payday loan should be off the table. They're simply unacceptable. Why? There are much cheaper options than paying 200 percent or more on a loan. With the massive amounts of credit cards in circulation, almost never should that type of loan be used. Remember, running to obtain a loan is all a consequence of our propagandized mind-set that fallaciously views borrowing as the *default* option, rather than a last resort.

The Pros and Cons of Paying with a Credit Card

As is the case with *everything*, using a credit card will have both pros and cons attached to it. Contrary to what those in the industry might tell you, the pros might entice you into a financially fattening situation but nonetheless may offer a benefit, and the cons might be less than you initially assumed.

The pros of using a credit card include the following:

- *Building Credit*: Having an established history of paying your bills in full and on time can help you improve your credit score. As we will later explain, *your credit score may not be everything it's cracked up to be.*
- *Ease of Payment*: Credit cards are obviously much easier to use than paper money, but some say they are almost *too* easy to use. If you are carrying revolving debt each month, every additional swipe means you are withdrawing from your future well-being.
- *Points and Benefits*: Being able to earn free flights, free vacations, and other desirable perks has helped perpetuate the credit card

industry. You must realize the card lenders are not offering you these perks because they're your friend—they want your money, and they know this is the best way to get it.

- *The Ability to Pay with Money You Haven't Yet Earned:* Credit cards make it possible to pay for things with money you have not yet earned. This can be great. It can also be terrible.

While credit card companies will try to claim that using their cards can produce other benefits, almost all benefits of credit cards can be boiled down into one of these four categories. Credit cards can be useful in certain situations, but they certainly have their fair share of risks:

- *Interest Costs:* Plenty of people put things on their card, planning to pay for them in the future. Perhaps it is our romantic sense of optimism about our future selves, but things do not always go quite as cleanly as initially planned.
- *Fees:* Credit card companies make a significant portion of their revenues via fees, of which there are certainly many. Under the guise of going green, some companies will even charge you for mailing your bill to your home—how convenient that it's always on Joe Six-pack to change and the onus is seldom on the lenders.
- *Cycles of Debt:* Having credit card debt is something that can quickly get out of hand. Once you owe one lender large amounts of money, you will likely need to borrow from another (usually at a higher interest rate) in order to make sure they are paid. Robbing Peter to pay Paul is a very common trap that can result in years of your own hard work being surrendered to someone else. Don't be like that elderly client who called in; perhaps 25 to 30 percent of his whole life's income was paid to interest on credit cards.

Don't let anyone tell you otherwise: using a credit card carries several unavoidable risks.

You may consider yourself to be a financially responsible person, and we have no reason to believe that you aren't. However, these traps have ruined the financial well-being of millions of people across the United States and elsewhere across the globe. Even if you are an excellent athlete, for example, that doesn't mean you should just willingly go rock climbing without any sort of support system. *Be aware of every financial risk that you take.*

Different Types of Credit

According to Experian, credit typically presents itself in four primary forms. Having debts in each of these forms can help improve your apparent credit mix, though again, having a good credit score alone does not mean that you are financially secure.

The four different types of credit include:

1. *Revolving Credit:* With a revolving line of credit, you will have a limited credit line that you can borrow against and pay back as you see fit (so long as you are complying with the lender's agreement). Most credit cards are revolving lines of credit, as well as most personal loans you can secure from a bank.
2. *Non-Revolving Charge Cards:* With this loan product, you must pay the total balance every month. In a way, these cards resemble revolving lines of credit, but they also contain an additional layer of "forced responsibility."
3. *Service Credit:* Any service that you receive on a regular basis, ranging from your gym membership to your internet service, will carry with it an implied line of credit. Though these services will typically not show up on your credit score, they are an indirect form of borrowing (receive Wi-Fi now, and pay for it at the end of the month).
4. *Installment Credit:* If you have made a major purchase, you will typically have the option to finance this purchase over time. Mortgages and car payments are two of the most common forms of installment credit.

Each of these types of credit will have certain risks and benefits associated with it. While it may not be reasonable to expect everyone to save up for their house in full by the time of purchase, thus avoiding interest payments for many years, it is reasonable to encourage people to avoid borrowing more than they can reasonably afford—something that is so common, especially with first-time buyers. Even if you need to carry a little bit of fat with you, that doesn't mean you need to let yourself go entirely.

Don't pursue credit just because it happens to improve your credit mix. If you are going to pursue credit, you need to have a clear plan to pay your debts back and also assure the total interest cost can be reasonably contained.

Deciding whether to Open or Close a Credit Card

If someone were to just blindly ask me, "Should I open an additional line of credit?" there would be no way for me to give a reasonable answer. The validity of opening any line of credit will depend on your personal circumstances, as well as the credit lines that are currently available. There are a few useful questions you can potentially ask yourself, however.

How much do I value having money in the status quo? The time value of money is something that is frequently discussed in the world of finance. If the cost of borrowing exceeds the benefits of borrowing, then opening a new line of credit does not make any sense.

What is my current credit situation? If you already have debts you've been unable to pay down, adding to this debt (usually with the soft self-promise "things will change") will almost always be counterproductive.

What is the purpose of opening another line of credit? You need to be honest with yourself about why you feel the need to borrow. Are you borrowing to help pay for your children's school supplies? Or are you borrowing for the sake of purchasing a new watch? Only you know the *real* answer to this question.

Credit cards can be great—when they are necessary. Unfortunately, they are typically not necessary, and they can create a wide range of financial problems. If you are someone who sincerely wants to trim the financial fat, looking at your credit card situation is the most obvious place for you to start.

Avoiding the Hazards of the Marketplace

It can be very easy for credit card companies to *"want"* to help you and act like they are your friend. After all, if you manage to shuffle several thousand dollars through their system, they may end up even giving you a free flight. Dealing with the credit card industry is something that needs to be approached with an exceptional degree of caution.

Assume these companies are trying to take advantage of you. They wouldn't be marketing to you if they didn't believe they'd profit from you. While it's true they kick back some benefits, they are often nominal benefits compared to all the interest you pay over time. In sum, there will be no one out there who is willing to hold your hand. It's up to you to hold your own.

CHAPTER 4

Buying a Car

As I created this chapter to help people use, manage, get out of, and even avoid excessive automotive debt, I spoke to my cousin who is the General Manager of the largest Toyota dealership in New England, an obvious expert in the automotive industry. He's literally in charge of marketing, sales, maintenance, repairs, and personnel - all while keeping track of thousands of vehicles coming in and out of his dealership on a monthly basis.

The information below, which has been contributed by my cousin, will serve as a "cheat sheet" for your next vehicle purchase.

Budgeting for a vehicle.

The question a buyer always considers is, "do I lease or do I buy?" For me it's very simple, when looking at vehicle you want to look at the lowest overall costs, including the lowest monthly payment. A longer term thought is how you can reserve an option of getting out of the vehicle without getting hit with exorbitant losses or even negative equity. Unless you're buying a classic, at the end of the road it's worth zero! It loses value and costs money every month and every year. A question I often asked myself for years is why people would buy something and then pay interest on it when its eventual value will be zero.

My suggestion is simple you either purchase a vehicle that is pre-owned or secondly lease a new vehicle.

When purchasing a pre-owned vehicle the first owner has already taken the biggest hit for the deprecation which typically occurs in the first 3 years. So you're buying vehicle with more value and lower cost than purchasing it new. It's possible at my dealership to find a 3 year old vehicle that will give years and years of reliable service that appears "new" at a price tag of about 60% of the cost of a new similar model. So with this purchase you save money right off the top, you have a lower monthly payment and lastly you finance less debt. Keeping a car like this for a decade or two is the financial ideal. However, for people that like to change their car every few years…

Leasing a vehicle is typically the true lowest monthly cost. Some dealerships offer leases of only $99 per month. Let's discuss the big myth about leasing…

I don't own it – the fact is that you don't own a vehicle if you financed it. The bank does. However, what you do own is the negative equity in the vehicle. On lease it falls 100% back on the bank. When the term of the lease is complete (generally in 2 or 3 years), you have options. It's possible to buy the vehicle for the residual value (the value of the vehicle that is set forth by the manufacturer), or you could trade it in and hopefully take advantage of any positive equity - if there is any and the get something new or new for you. Lastly, you can simply give it back to the bank and then decide later if/when you want to get another vehicle. The simple fact is that you have options, but on a purchase the average loan is 72 months - so after 3 years you still have 3 more years of payments.

Let's talk about money – a general rule of thumb on financing is that your payment will be $200 per month for every 10k financed. The average vehicle costs 30k these days which equates to an estimated payment of $600 - a lot of money for a struggling consumer. On lease, typically your payment runs $100 to $150 less per month than the financed amount because you are only paying toward a portion of the vehicle's total value. For example, if the vehicle is 30k and the residual is 15k your lease payment over 36 months is based on the 15k difference not the whole 30k. Your payment is based on sale price less the residual value. Furthermore, your payment over 36 months before interest is about $277 per month, whereas the typical financed payment would be about $600 per month. What about miles? I drive too many! The good news is that you can negotiate and tailor a lease to your driving habits and set the lease to cap out at any number miles that you think you need. Most manufactures charge you 10 cents a mile up front and 15 cents per mile if you exceed the agreed mileage threshold. Lastly, keep in mind if you choose not to lease the same car again or purchase it outright, most dealers will charge you a $350 disposal fee. Be aware and careful of all these numbers before signing. Other than that you're good to go.

Jason Aufiero
Boch Toyota
General Manager

If someone were to tell you to "picture a car salesman," what is the first image that comes to your mind?

If you are an optimist, you might be picturing a well-meaning individual who simply makes a living trying to help people get around town.

If you're a realist, on the other hand, you are likely picturing someone who is going to give you less than you asked for, at a price that was greater than you anticipated.

We are not saying there is no such thing as an honest, good, or ethical car salesman. However, because car dealers are selling products worth four, five, or even six figures, the industry itself is one that is ripe for manipulation. As we have discussed with mortgages and credit cards, it can be very easy for a salesman to dupe you into a bad deal. Once again, you'll find yourself carrying more fat than your financial body simply needs.

Many people having confidence to negotiate the price of a car will walk away from their final handshake with a proud smile on their face. After all, he was asking for $20,000 and you were able to "talk him down" all the way to $19,500, plus a fresh set of tires. While keeping the five hundred dollars in your pocket is certainly something to be excited about, you *also* gave away $19,500 of your own free will. Was this a good deal? What does a good deal even look like?

The car-dealing industry can be incredibly deceptive, as you might expect. It is almost always in the dealer's best interest to cover up the "whole" truth. Even if you agree to pay the sticker price, this is very rarely the total amount you will end up paying. People look at a twenty-thousand-dollar car and think, "I am making a twenty-thousand-dollar investment." They consider the situation to be as simple and unadulterated as setting aside twenty thousand dollars for their retirement savings.

In reality, the sticker price is only one simple component of what you will end up paying for the car. As is the case with any major financial investment you are currently considering, you will need to do a total and comprehensive analysis of the situation before making any firm commitments.

Remember, it is the dealer who needs *your* money in order to make a living. You, on the other hand, do not need to go to any specific dealer or make any specific deal in order to purchase a car. You are the one who has seemingly limitless options. You, as the consumer, are the one who holds the power.

Don't let anyone ever tell you otherwise.

The Total Cost of Owning a Car

Due to various cultural, economic, and historical factors, the United States has among the highest car ownership rates of any country in the world. Does this mean that everyone who owns a car can realistically afford one? Absolutely not. Does this mean that every car owner decided on a car that was within their price range? Again, absolutely not.

As you likely know by now, owning a car actually has many different financial components. While a healthy budget will be able to categorize each of these components individually, it is still important for you to remember that they are all coming from the same source.

1. *Insurance:* Most decent insurance plans, even if you are purchasing a used car, will cost around one hundred dollars per month or even more. Using this figure, you can expect to pay at least twelve hundred dollars per year on car insurance. If you own the car for five years, then you will end up paying upward of six thousand dollars.
2. *Gas:* Gas prices change quite often, and your total fuel expenses will depend on how and how much you end up driving (as well as your vehicle's fuel efficiency). Generally speaking, this is another expense that often exceeds one hundred dollars per month. You can expect to pay another six thousand dollars over the course of five years.

3. *Taxes, Registration, and Other Fees:* Depending on where you live, your car can be considered taxable property and will subject you to an annual property tax. In some places, you might be further burdened with a sales tax that can be upward of 10 percent of the total cost of the car—this represents a potential one thousand dollars-plus fee that many people end up overlooking.

4. *Maintenance and Repairs:* These will obviously vary tremendously depending on the current condition and performance of your car. Some months, you may need to end up paying several thousand dollars. Other months, you will not need to pay anything at all. When averaged over five years, you can typically expect to pay at least three thousand dollars in total maintenance costs.

5. *Interest:* Depending on the car loan you secure, it is realistic that the amount you pay in interest will be more than 20 percent of the total cost of the car. However, unlike some of the other variables included in this list, this is a cost of car ownership that can potentially be reduced.

Add this all up, and it becomes obvious that owning a car is much more "fattening" than many people initially assume. Working off this fat will take a considerable amount of time. For the interest of your future self, save yourself the trouble and begin by making disciplined choices *up front.*

Even looking at this simple list—which still doesn't account for *everything*—it is clear that the total cost of owning a car is likely much more than expected. In fact, recent estimates from AAA indicate that the average car ownership costs $8,469 per year, *in addition to* the principal payment. There are quite a few ways you can lower this initial figure. It is important to note that after your eyes light up when seeing the sticker price of the car you buy, you are still going to need to pay a lot of money.

Even if you could be given a car for free, these costs cannot be ignored.

How to Budget for a Car

Once you have been able to account for the *total* cost of owning a car, budgeting for a car should be a little bit easier. However, we are yet to answer the initial underlying question: *How do you know you are buying a car you can afford? How do you know you are getting a good deal?*

Naturally, trusted resources such as Kelley Blue Book (KBB) are among the most useful ways to determine what a specific car is worth. Additionally, you should ask for reports on the car and try to determine whether this car should be sold above or below the expected KBB value. This is only the beginning of the budgeting process. You will need to account for your personal situation as well.

The *total cost* of owning a car priced at twenty thousand dollars, financed over the course of five years, can often be upward of sixty thousand dollars—triple the sticker price! Considering that this figure is actually *greater than* the median household income in the United States, this is certainly no small chunk of change. Spending 20 percent of your income on your car is the equivalent of dedicating ten workweeks to that cost alone.

As is the case when creating any budget, you should allow for some wiggle room in the event of unexpected costs (such as damages not covered by insurance). As a general rule of thumb, you should spend between 10 and 20 percent of your after-tax income on your car. Suppose that your take-home income is fifty thousand dollars per year. Over the course of five years, you will earn $250,000.

Using the 20 percent rule, this means that the most you can realistically spend *on everything* related to the car is ten thousand dollars per year. At this rate, a twenty-thousand-dollar car will be *barely* within your price range. If you need to pay for parking, something that is common for urban dwellers, this will also need to be accounted for. Even just fifty dollars per month in parking costs will balloon to three thousand dollars over the course of five years.

In other words, even individuals who are comfortably in the middle class will need to be careful with the amount they spend on an automobile. Just as we recommend when you are considering purchasing a home, you should always lean on the side of caution and *buy less* than you think you can afford.

Yes, all things considered, a car can be considered a necessary expense.

But did you need to buy the Cadillac instead of the Chevrolet?

And while we are at it, did you need to buy the new Chevrolet instead of a used Chevrolet?

Those involved in the car industry will consistently tell you that any car more than five years old is practically a dinosaur. However, advancing technologies have made it possible for *many* cars to comfortably make it up to two hundred fifty thousand miles. Making it to one hundred thousand miles is even more of a reasonable goal. So while you may have splurged in order to cover this very necessary expense, it is important to realize which portions of this expense were necessary and which portions were spent out of vanity.

Finding Ways to Reduce Costs

As we stated earlier, there are many different factors contained in the total cost of owning a car. Within each of these components, you can find ways that you can possibly save on the total cost of buying a car.

1. *Insurance:* While you should probably avoid purchasing the state minimum, there is a significant difference between the minimum and the amount that most insurance agents say is actually necessary. After a careful risk calculation, cutting a few of the superfluous perks in your insurance policy is a great way to begin trimming the financial fat.
2. *Gas:* This is a component of owning a car that is seemingly inevitable—however, purchasing a fuel-efficient car is about a lot more than saving the environment. It can also help you

save on an otherwise unpleasant (and sometimes unpredictable) monthly cost.

3. *Taxes, Registration, and Other Fees:* Purchasing a car in certain geographic areas can help you potentially avoid (or at least decrease) the sales tax you will be expected to pay.

4. *Maintenance and Repairs:* While these costs are sometimes avoidable, they can still be prepared for. Beyond your insurance policy, you should set aside a little bit of money each month in order to cover you from unexpected expenses. This way, you will not need to repair your car and also pay the cost of repaid interest.

5. *Interest:* This is the portion of owning a car that can be most easily controlled. Applying for a shorter car loan will increase your monthly payments, but it will significantly reduce the amount you pay overall. By saving as much as you can in advance and purchasing a reasonably priced car, you can significantly reduce the amount of money that you are *willingly handing to the bank!*

Additionally, it goes without saying, purchasing used cars instead of new cars is one of the most effective ways for you to save money. The *first mile* after a car is driven off a lot can reduce its value by potentially thousands of dollars. Nothing has fundamentally changed about this car except for the fact it has had an owner, on paper. If you are willing to accept that someone has driven your car before, you will be able to get a deal that is, proportionately speaking, much more justifiable on paper.

It will also be important for you to do plenty of research in advance. You should walk into the dealership with a hard figure in mind. Suppose that you determine model X by Y maker from Z year is worth ten thousand dollars. When you walk into the dealer and they tell you the asking price for this car is twelve thousand dollars, you will have several options.

You could accept that your calculations were "wrong" and pay more than you initially planned. Many people go down this path because they are tired, desire to avoid confrontations, and adhere to the false notion that the "dealer must be right." This is the equivalent of giving up during the most important part of your workout. Nobody will ever get financially fit this way. Instead, you can attempt to negotiate the price of the car and move it toward a reasonable range. Or you could leave.

The car dealer will do everything they can to avoid you leaving or paying less than they asked for. This is when it is especially important for you to remember that *as the customer, you have the power.* You can live without them, while they cannot live without you. This relationship, contrary to how the dealer may frame it, is entirely lopsided.

It will also be critical for you to try to establish a positive relationship with the dealer. Car sales associates' commission on a car is much lower than what most people think. When on a test ride, telling the salesperson that you are on their side (and even offering a tip of one hundred dollars before the deal is finalized for excellent service and the price that you want) may help inspire them to level with you and work within your actual budget. The one-hundred-dollar tip could save you two thousand dollars or more, so that's money well spent.

Again, as was the case with buying a house, trimming the financial fat and improving your financial fitness is all about recognizing what you need and what you don't need. It will be up to you to make the final decision. If you are honest with yourself, you can save a considerable amount of money. Do your future self a favor and cut the cost of debt before it has a chance to cut you.

Preparing to Sell Your Car

The final component of owning a car is preparing to sell that car. Even if the car is completely inoperable, there will likely be someone nearby willing to give you *something* for it.

As is the case with reselling anything, it will be important to do so with an *opportunity cost* perspective. With each potential upgrade you are considering, you should think about the financial impact that would have on the car.

If it costs five hundred dollars to fix something on your car and this fix will add four hundred dollars to its total value, obviously this fix is something you should probably forgo. Where do you draw the line? Is $501 of value worth paying five hundred dollars to fix? If you value your time, probably not. What about six hundred dollars? Six hundred fifty dollars?

This is the exact sort of mind-set you should have when selling a car, selling a home, or selling anything else of significant value. The choices that are right for you will obviously depend on your specific situation. Regardless, making the effort to financially account for *each and every* detail can have a tremendous impact on your financial situation.

The Final Drive

Again, we hope that you do not read this chapter thinking that we are against the prospect of car ownership. Owning a car can be a great thing and, in a sense, represents its own form of financial freedom. However, what we are against is the prospect of *owning a car you cannot afford.* As you walk around the dealership and see the options you have available, it can be very tempting to want to buy now and pay later. Remember, any benefit you are accelerating into the status quo is something you are taking away from your future self. By being realistic and understanding this complex market, you can work within your budget, while still getting a reasonable ride.

CHAPTER 5

Credit Score Myths

If you have paid attention to any credit-related advertisements over the past few years, you have probably noticed the apparent *obsession* with credit scores. While having a good credit score is undeniably a valuable thing, it is really just one small component of what is an otherwise much larger financial picture.

Your financial profile is made up of many different things. Your credit score just so *happens* to be one of these things.

In this chapter, we will discuss the most important things for you to know about your credit score. While we will not dispute that having a good credit score can be valuable, we will specifically discuss credit score myths. Creditors are the greatest peddlers of fat in the industry; if you only listen to their advice, you will inevitably find yourself bloated, even unable to move.

We will also discuss the importance of remembering that your credit score is simply a *means* to an end. This end, of course, is a state of financial stability. If you ever find yourself in a situation where pursuing a better credit score requires you making yourself financially *worse off* for the time being—and these situations come about far more often than most lenders care to admit—you should stop and think. Why are you even applying for a specific loan in the first place?

- What is the purpose of borrowing?
- What is the purpose of assuming additional debt?
- What is the purpose of willingly making yourself less free?

Though there is no denying that credit is indeed *sometimes* necessary, it is not nearly as important as many in the industry would claim. Do you really need to change your oil every five thousand miles? Mechanics—individuals who at least partially rely on people changing their oil in order for them to make a living—would likely tell you yes. On the other hand, most experienced car owners would tell you, depending on the age, make and model, you could wait seventy-five hundred miles or even more before changing your oil. The mechanic would then tell you it is better to be safe than sorry, which, while generally good advice, is also an easy way of convincing people to use their services more often.

The credit industry works the exact same way. Is it really necessary for you to have five active lines of credit open at once? This may, after all, have a marginally positive impact on your credit score, depending on how these lines of credit are managed. Consider this: those who rely on promoting lines of credit in order to make a living will often hold high credit scores in *disproportionately* high regard. There will always be an "apparent" benefit that can come from borrowing more, setting up decades-long payment plans, and obsessing over your credit score.

This notion, the radical idea that anything that is good for your credit score must be good for the borrower, is what we describe as the *credit card myth*. The sooner you can liberate yourself from these tired, almost criminally misleading lines of logic, the sooner you will be able to regain total control of your personal finances. While we will discuss a few of the ways you can potentially improve your credit score (again, not necessarily a bad idea), there is one clear and undeniable way you can reduce the impact of having a less-than-perfect score: stop treating credit as the *end-all, be-all* that life exists in pursuit of.

For some, credit is a means to an end. Nothing more. Living the good life will require something much deeper than three digits on a cheap piece of paper.

Understanding Your Credit Score

What is the purpose of a credit score?

Credit scores have, without a doubt, established themselves as a major component of the banking and lending industries. The *clear* purpose of a credit score is to make it easier for lenders to determine your general ability to repay a loan. After all, in a nation where there is no such thing as a debtor's prison, if you have had an extended history of borrowing money and not paying your lenders back, new lenders will want to be aware of this. Justifiably so, lenders will compensate themselves with much higher interest rates attached to the loans for the risks they are assuming. Without some method of evaluating a potential borrower's lendability, all borrowers would be forced to accept the same high-interest rates.

Fair enough.

However, there is a deeper and less self-evident purpose of having a credit score as well. The credit score, according to credit marketers, is essentially an extension of *the self*. It plays into a consumer's hubris and gives them a sensation they're better than the next person due to their high credit score, notwithstanding all other financial elements such as total debt amount owed, cash on hand, and so on ... If your FICO is 750 and you're living paycheck to paycheck and the next person is a millionaire with a FICO score of 650, who is better off? This flawed mind-set encouraged by the lending industry creates an excellent opportunity for pushing additional lines of credit. This is the hidden purpose of a credit score, which, likely deliberately created for this reason, has had a major impact on the industry as a whole.

Many people unwittingly assume that their credit score is an official figure. One that may even be closely monitored and kept track of by the federal government, comparable to the amount of money you have contributed to social security. After all, the term *FICO* sounds even more official and bureaucratic than terms like Fannie Mae and Freddie Mac.

FICO, in actuality, is merely an abbreviation for *Fair, Isaac, and Company* (named after the company's founders Bill Fair and Earl Isaac). This entirely private company, created in the 1950s, makes its revenue (nearly $1 billion per year) by selling FICO credit scores. Experian and Equifax—both very official-sounding company names as well—operate in a very similar arena.

By creating this apparent "credit score industrial complex," it becomes much easier for banks to dictate which behaviors can be deemed as *good* and which behaviors can be deemed as *bad*. Taking out a huge loan and making the minimum payments (which are, coincidentally, very expensive for you over time and mostly interest) for thirty consecutive years—in the eyes of the credit industry—makes you a model citizen. Over time, doing this will almost certainly give you a much better credit score.

Saving up for your major purchases and only paying for things with money you've already earned—in the eyes of the credit industry—makes you an outcast, a financial reject, someone who likely has something seriously wrong with them. You're an individual who has not bought into the system, and as a result, your credit score will be far from high.

As you can see, *actually* being financially responsible, even wealthy, and having a high credit score are not strongly correlated with one another. In the examples above, when all else is equal, the careful saver who spends minimally and avoids financing is clearly the one who has developed better financial habits. However, the person willing to shackle themselves in debt—as long as they make the minimum payments—will end up having a much better score.

Lenders will always recommend that you should borrow more and borrow for longer periods of time. They need to make a living somehow, after all. It will remain up to you to choose whether or not you listen to them.

Navigating the Credit Market

If you are hoping to enter into the credit market, it will be important for you to tread carefully and be at least somewhat skeptical of *everything* you are told. If there *is* an offer that is financially in your best interest to accept, that offer will remain on the table even after you have had a chance to go home and think about it.

There are five different components of your FICO credit score:

1. *Payment History (35 percent):* Your payment history will include almost every sort of borrowing you've done in the past, including mortgages, student loans, car loans, and various others. If you have an established history of paying back your debts in full and on time, you will be considered to be more lendable.
2. *Credit Utilization (30 percent):* This factor considers both the amount you are currently *allowed* to be borrowing as well as the amount you have *actually* borrowed. Having a major gap between your borrowing levels and the amount you can, theoretically, borrow will have a positive impact on your overall score. However, there are quite a few unexpected complications that can result from wide credit utilization gaps.
3. *Length of Credit History (15 percent):* If your credit accounts have been open for longer, this will have a positive impact on your score. This makes sense, due to the fact it means your credit history is more established. However, this portion of the score makes it much easier for lenders to insist that your accounts remain open and that you remain an active customer—you know, "for your own good."
4. *New Credit (10 percent):* If most of your accounts are brand-new (for example, you opened multiple accounts in a month), this will have an overall negative impact on your credit score. Of all the categories, this is the one that probably encourages financial responsibility the most.

5. *Credit Mix (10 percent):* Having multiple different types of credit will make lenders believe you are a more lendable individual. Coincidentally, many banks will use this as an opportunity to encourage multiple different types of borrowing.

And that's it.

These five factors are the only components that go into calculating your credit score. As you can see, there are multiple marketing opportunities built in to the scoring process. Lenders will always have the motivation to tell you that you should borrow more, borrow for longer, and borrow different types of credit.

They are not lying when they say these things will eventually help your credit score, at least to a certain extent. But you cannot forget the importance of asking yourself, *What are you borrowing for in the first place? Is it just so you will be able to borrow even more money at a lower rate in the future?*

Common Credit Score Myths

When people talk about credit score myths, the most common myth that will come to mind is the notion that *checking your score will lower your credit.* However, in the current year of this book being published, this opinion is not true. There are multiple ways to check your credit score (mostly online) for free, and this will not hurt your credit. The scores reported online are simply *rough estimates.* In exchange for giving you these estimates for free—surprise, surprise—you will have to endure marketing material from various lenders and credit companies.

While this myth has long been debunked, it is really only the beginning of a long line of misleading statements perpetuated throughout the credit industry. We are *constantly* being inundated with credit score myths, and falling for some of these myths can be detrimental to our long-term financial health.

Here are some of the most common credit score myths you may have heard:

1. *Employers check your credit scores:* This is yet another way that your credit score is propped up to be much more important than it actually is. Unless you have authorized your employer to check, doing so is actually against the law. For this reason, most employers altogether avoid this practice.

2. *Bad credit scores mean you will not be able to borrow:* The threat of not being able to secure a mortgage in the future is one of the many things lenders use to encourage people to keep playing their game. Nevertheless, many people can close on a mortgage with a credit score of 580 or even worse. Can you believe that? Yet even with this being said, down payment requirements have also been decreasing.

3. *It takes seven years to improve a bad credit score:* As a general rule of thumb, any claim that it takes seven years to resolve an issue should immediately be taken with a grain of salt. As a child, you were probably told it takes seven years for your stomach to digest gum (something that has no scientific support whatsoever). Credit companies benefit from the fact that, out of fear of long-term consequences, people will never test their credit limits. Credit reporting is dynamic, based on many factors and changing often within just a short period of time. While you should be responsible with your borrowing habits, painting a broad brush to include all situations under the seven year rule is logically flawed, and this myth is obviously baseless.

4. *Debt is required to build a good credit score:* If you *are* hoping to improve your credit score—for whatever reason—you should not assume that massive debt is an absolute necessity. One good strategy for building credit is something I like to call a "gum card." Each month, use your credit card to buy one small item, such as a pack of gum. Once you have made this purchase, pay off your debt, put the card back in your drawer, and wait until the next month comes around. This will help you improve

your credit score while limiting your amount of debt to a dollar or two.

Many involved in the credit industry are aware that these credit score myths are consistently circling about, but few are willing to actually do anything about it. The companies always tend to be pro fat in the status quo, assuming you can resolve this issue later. When the public's misperceptions of a product happen to help your bottom line, it can be difficult to try to do the right thing and correct public opinion.

Most credit score myths—and the list above contains just a few—are centered upon the same old and tired mantras:

- *You must keep borrowing.*
- *You must keep paying us back.*
- *Open more lines of credit, and we will reward you.*

Again, the industry seems to have the entire thing backward. *They* are not rewarding *you*; *you* are rewarding *them*. Typically this reward comes in the form of borrowing with interest rates much higher than can be found on the stock market. Lenders will happily let you accumulate thousands of dollars of interest debt, only to "graciously" throw you a bone in the future by way of a gift card or a few points.

Those issues are even worse when it comes to lenders offering payday loans (something that should be avoided at all costs) and other forms of predatory lending. These loans are not designed for any person to reasonably ever pay back. But if a lender can offer a ten thousand dollar loan, allow that debt to inflate to one hundred thousand dollars, and then "settle" with a debt relief agency for fifty thousand dollars, they will have made an easy forty thousand dollar profit. Do this multiple times per week, and you have an easy path to becoming a millionaire.

Remember, it is the responsibility of the borrower to be aware of any contract they are entering into. However, to think that the lenders in these stories are somehow victims who have been ripped off is preposterous. Though this view may sound unnecessarily cynical, whenever you are navigating the ebbs and flows of the credit market, you should *always* assume that lenders are trying to take advantage of you, and you should *always* take extra care trying to look out for yourself. Remember:

1. If you are to go swimming with the sharks, it will be important for you to tread lightly.
2. At the first whiff of blood, they'll bite.

Preparing Yourself for the Future

At this point in the chapter, you are probably thinking to yourself, "I get that the credit industry can be dangerous, but do I really have any other options?" There are, after all, some situations where people have no choice but to borrow. Student loans are a prime example of this. If you need to go to trade school or college in order to obtain the career of your dreams, you will need to first borrow money in order to make the money needed to pay it back.

However, conceding the point that credit is sometimes necessary *should not* open the door to the idea that all lines of credit can be justified. In fact, though there is likely no scientific way to test this, I believe it is incredibly likely that the *majority* of all lines of credit in the United States were not in any way close to actually being necessary.

I think back to a time when I was recently on a plane coming home from a trade show. Shortly before landing, the flight attendants walked down the aisle, trying to convince as many people as they could to sign up for a credit card that could help them accumulate more miles and points. Of the people I could reasonably see from my seat—and I kid you not—roughly one in four began filling out the paperwork needed to apply for a card. Roughly half accepted at least a brochure explaining the program further.

You have likely noticed similar events in your own life. Presumably, *none* of these people got onto the plane planning to open another line of credit. After all, if they were really such frequent fliers and this was really such a good deal, they would have likely already signed up for the card. Yet the quarter of the population that signed up for that plan was swayed—with minimal prompting—and consequently made major changes to their credit situation.

Maybe they didn't want to be rude to the flight attendant (the same reason I would buy a box of Girl Scout cookies from a kid going door-to-door, even though I don't like foods high in sugar).

Perhaps they were planning on opening a line of credit anyway.

More likely than not, these were just normal people who allowed the credit industry to trample their sense of financial independence. These sorts of events happen every day, across the country and throughout the world.

If you are preparing for the future, there are a few basic principles you should try to keep in mind:

1. Never consider borrowing to be the *default option.*
2. You probably don't need nearly as much to get by as you initially assume.
3. Love your future self. How many minutes per day are you willing to force your future self to work in order to make sure you have something glorious in the present? Why does the present self always get to be the lazy one?
4. If it's possible to save for something, do it.
5. If it's possible to pay in full, do it.
6. Having a higher credit score will not make you happy or better than the next person. While at times this score may be financially convenient, happiness is a human objective that— without a doubt—lies in something much more profound.

While these insights have been self-evident to many people, they are also facts of life that the credit industry is actively trying to suppress. Deep down, you *know* what you need and what can be considered a luxury; you *know* whether borrowing from your future self is actually needed in the status quo; you *know* that credit is just an illusion, an arrangement, a way of rearranging your obligations in life.

With these nuggets of knowledge in hand, it will be impossible for the credit industry to bring you down.

The Bottom Line

So far, this book has been a long journey. Beginning with the first few steps, it became immediately apparent that the long road to financial fitness does not lie upon the path that most people initially assume.

Financial freedom involves so much more than consistently borrowing from lenders and paying your loans back on time. Fitness, of any kind, requires work. If anyone promises you that they can offer an easy fix or a guaranteed solution to your problems, they are not even worth the snake oil they're selling.

We are not saying that trekking along this road will be easy. Langston Hughes's poem "Mother to Son" is certainly one that comes to mind. But if you are able to take a step back, take a deep breath, realize what you actually need, and take control of your own destiny, financial freedom is something that is well within your reach.

And once you are there, oh, once you are there—you will realize that the long road less traveled was undeniably worth it.

CHAPTER 6

Escaping the Debt Trap

By now, it should be obvious that there are, in fact, many ways for you to potentially avoid debt entrapment. Despite the fact that millions of Americans have already found themselves holding debts they simply cannot afford, exercising discipline can still put you on a path toward long-term financial security. There is no amount of personal financial fat in the status quo that cannot, eventually, be overcome.

As you will find when trying to pursue any personal fitness goal, creating a genuine state of financial security is not something that will simply happen overnight. It will take hard work. It will take consistency. And most of all, it will certainly require making many sacrifices along the way.

However, while the possibility of financial security may be clear to some people, it is not uncommon for people to find themselves holding too much debt to bear. Even after cutting out as many expenses as you possibly can, your debt may still exceed your entire income altogether. When this is the case, maintaining a constant sense of discipline will not be enough. Even if you could commit *100 percent* of your income to paying down your debts, you may discover that these debts are relentlessly growing over time.

If you are deep in debt and the guidelines offered in this book are not yet enough to make a difference, you may find yourself looking for some immediate solutions.

As of 2018, the collective American public carries nearly $14 trillion worth of debt. This figure is greater than 60 percent of the annual national GDP, indicating that, at least at the household level, major changes are needed. If you are one of the many people who finds themselves carrying this burden, you will be looking for ways to completely restructure your debt altogether.

Breaking Down the Components of Debt

Debt is a complex animal; as you quickly discover, there are many different components of ordinary consumer debt. Unsurprisingly, this creates a situation where there are also many different possible solutions available.

The most relevant components of consumer debt include:

- *Term Length:* The term length is the amount of time that, if things go according to plan, you will have to pay back your debts. When your debt is structured with a relatively long term length, you will not need to pay as much each month. However, due to the compounding effects of interest, loans with longer term lengths will require you to pay more overall.
- *Interest Rate:* The interest rate (often quoted in terms of APY or APR) is the amount that your debt is growing with each passing year. Essentially, the interest rate represents the overall cost of borrowing. If you already have a poor credit situation, then any additional loans will require you to pay a much higher interest rate. In theory, this should shift the risk-reward ratio against the pursuit of additional credit. However, in a state of desperation, many people ignore this ratio and instead choose to pursue a clearly temporary solution.
- *Monthly Payments:* This figure represents how much you will actually need to pay on a monthly basis. As you would expect,

the monthly payment is directly tied to both your interest rate and the term length of your debt(s).

- *Total Debt:* This figure represents the net sum of all sources of debt. Regardless of your situation, your total debts are something that—eventually—you are going to need to take active steps to reduce.

If you do hope to make your debt more manageable, at least one of these components will need to be directly altered. It is true that expanding the term length may give you a little bit of relief in the status quo. However, because your debt will have a greater number of periods to compound over, this will make the debt itself much more dangerous to be holding on to.

In some situations, you may be able to directly renegotiate the interest rate you are paying on your loan. However, if you have already overextended your debt and your credit score is already suffering, these negotiations may not be as fruitful as you initially hoped. The solutions you are looking for may need to be found elsewhere.

Ultimately, reducing your *total debt* will be the most desirable option available. As your total amount of debt is reduced, your monthly payments and the impacts of interest rates (on the principal) will also be reduced as well.

Reducing the total amount you owe to lenders is undoubtedly the most desirable option available. The next thing you will need to figure out is how *exactly* this can eventually be accomplished.

The Pros and Cons of Consumer Credit Counseling Services

According to the Federal Deposit Insurance Corporation (FDIC), the consumer credit counseling industry has assisted as many as 4 million people manage their debts per year—roughly 2 percent of the adult population. These programs attempt to work directly with creditors in order to find a solution that, ultimately, can be deemed acceptable to both parties.

Generally speaking, consumer credit counseling services will attempt to renegotiate the various terms such as payment due dates or interest rates attached to each of your enrolled debts. However, many of these negotiations are attached to their own set of consequences. For example, while they may be able to help reduce the interest amount that you're paying, they may end up extending the length of (and perhaps consequently increasing the total cost of) your loan. You need to evaluate the circumstances on a case by case basis.

A possible benefit of using consumer credit counseling services is that they can reduce the term of your loan. When pressed against the wall looking at thirty years of credit card payments, reducing your term to seven years is undeniably a very valuable thing.

If you're living at or close to paycheck to paycheck, these solutions are largely a Band-Aid rather than a truly sustainable solution because these programs don't address the root of the problem, cash flow. The industry wide reality is that more than half of the consumers that join a credit counseling program actually fallout due to the unsustainability of the monthly payments. In sum, you are hardly losing your financial fat; rather, you are putting on a financial waist trainer which merely gives a temporary financial solution to look better in the mirror. However, if you're dealing with limited means, the same end result arises over time, the realization that the change was only a temporary unsuccessful solution that made you feel good at the time.

You have not resolved your debts; you have merely *rearranged* the ways in which they will be paid off. As months or years go by and your monthly payments continue to remain, you run the risk of exhausting any savings you may have, and you will realize that these sorts of solutions may not be everything they originally claimed to be.

If you truly hope to escape debt entrapment, you will need to look for a service that can attack the core issue; without directly addressing the principal amount of debt, for many these solutions are—at best—temporary.

Finding Solutions via Debt Settlement Programs

As stated above, the four different components of debt include the interest rate, the monthly payment, the term length, and the total principal. If you want to resolve your debt in a way that is genuine and truly sustainable, you will need to directly confront these components *without* causing the other components to increase to your overall detriment.

Decreasing monthly payments while increasing the overall principal is not *truly* an effective debt relief solution.

Decreasing future interest rates without decreasing the overall monthly payment is not *truly* a debt relief solution.

Decreasing the total principal owed, while also decreasing total monthly payments and even decreasing the overall term length or interest rate, may be a solution that is worth pursuing.

While on its face, they both seem related, consumer credit counseling services and debt settlement programs have very different underlying modes of debt relief, and in some cases, they even directly compete against each other.

Consumer credit counseling services can offer modifications to your term length by reducing your interest rates, and can at time change other mild components of your debt. Debt settlement services, on the other hand, can save you from bankruptcy and directly attack your debt head-on.

With a debt settlement company, your debt can be cut in half or even more. After a series of negotiations and overall debt restructuring, you may quickly see seventy-five thousand dollars worth of debt, which might have a total cost of two hundred thousand dollars or more over time, reduced to about thirty-five thousand dollars or less!

Debt settlement programs will rarely (if ever) resolve you of all your debt entirely. Why? Because there are excluded debts, such as a home or an automobile. But after watching your monthly payments decrease by 50 percent or even more—without a corresponding increase in term length—you can roll some of the savings forward toward other debts, such as a home or automobile. You will soon realize that these solutions are indeed among the most sustainable.

As you will find with any solution to your financial problems, the benefits of debt settlement programs are not delivered without a few corresponding trade-offs. Your credit score will almost always take a hit, which, in turn, will make it more difficult to secure any additional sources of debt during the interim of the program. Keep in mind, though, it's your debt that's holding you back and taking money out of your monthly budget each month, not your credit score.

Again, if you are already deeply in debt, your credit score is likely far from perfect. And while your credit score is merely an abstract figure that *may* impact your financial health further down the line, your debt is a material reality that is directly affecting your financial well-being with each passing day in the status quo.

Your credit score, at its face, is not equivalent to wealth. If you have no plans on borrowing in the future, then your credit score is little more than a vain (and inaccurate) representation of past financial decisions. There are many people who have a great credit score who do not have a net worth exceeding ten thousand dollars, and millionaires do exist with average or even poor credit scores. So while having a great credit score may be "nice," it is certainly a far cry from something that needs to be a top priority when cutting financial fat *and becoming financially fit*. With this in mind, the benefits of pursuing a debt settlement program will almost always outweigh the benefits of consumer credit counseling services.

Another associated risk with a debt settlement service is the small chance that a creditor might file a claim against you in court. Keep in mind though, just because a claim is filed it doesn't mean they automatically win their day in court. When you're seeking a service like this, it's not a form of a communication to the creditor stating that you're totally unwilling to pay. The reality is that you cannot afford to pay the balance in full with all the associated interest. Creditors often have to deal with consumers that show no manifestation to resolve the debt, for example a non-paying consumer that changes his telephone number often and tries to play the "cat and mouse game." So for the fact that you're making an effort and funds are being designated each month for negotiation it puts you in a position to settle the claim. Even a mutually designed payment plan for the balance in full is better than a payment plan with no end in sight. Perhaps the savings won't be the best, but robbing Peter to pay Paul for 30 years isn't either!

Resolving Debt and Starting Over

By pursuing a debt settlement program, you are moving one step closer to resolving your persistent and relentless debt issues. In this long trek toward a state of financial fitness, you are mending your broken bones, resolving to eat healthier (throwing out the fat in favor of something that keeps you energized), and taking small steps toward creating a lifestyle that can feasibly be sustained over time.

When deciding whether pursuing a debt settlement program is objectively in your best interest, ask yourself the following questions:

- *Are the benefits of maintaining my current state of debt greater than the benefits of making a change and starting anew?*
- *What is my current credit score? Can I actually justify taking out any additional loans in the future? If my credit score will not impact my future well-being, why do I consider it to be so fundamentally important?*

- *What percentage of my income is being directed toward paying off debts? Of this percentage, how much is being directed toward interest payments?*
- *What are my long-term financial objectives? If given a chance to start over, what can I do differently to turn these dreams into realities?*

Exhausted by years of outstanding debts, you may feel hopeless. You may feel that, because you are in debt, then debt must be a permanent part of your life. However, in the pursuit of financial fitness, nothing could be further from the truth. Your debt is not an irreversible part of who you are—it is merely a reflection of your current state. Just as a runner's broken bones can inevitably be mended, your debts are something that can inevitably be resolved.

Once you are walking again, you will realize that this was a change worth making.

The Joys of Living a Debt-Free Lifestyle

Webster defines Stockholm syndrome as "feelings of trust or affection felt in many cases of kidnapping or hostage-taking by a victim toward a captor." After being entrapped for so long, many individuals will begin to believe that their state of entrapment is something that is entirely natural and even deserved. While debt may not be quite the same thing as a hostage situation, many individuals who are deeply in debt begin to experience highly comparable feelings.

As consumers, we are all too often held hostage by the idea that debt is the natural, default state of being. We defend our current practices because, being surrounded by an industry that seeks to perpetuate debt by all means necessary, the possibility of living a debt-free lifestyle is something that seems foreign and unattainable.

At best, debt is something that can give us access to future earnings in the status quo. When it comes to owning a house or buying a car, this may occasionally be necessary. But even then, the level of debts that consumers take on in order to live the so-called good life is far beyond what can be justified on paper. And more importantly, these debts do not come without an immediate cost.

At worst, debt is a form of self-inflicted shackling that makes living the good life fundamentally impossible. People will work sixty-hour weeks and demand a raise only to see their funds redirected to lenders who did little more than push themselves in the right place at the right time. *Debt* is so rarely the fundamental enabler of a happy life. Instead, debt is an almost cancerous disease. When left untreated, it will continue to grow, draining the consumer of their own financial health and, in some cases, even their basic sense of dignity.

There may not be an end-all, be-all cure to this cancerous disease, but there are certainly reasonable treatments available. Even if your current debts cannot be entirely resolved with a single push of a button, they can certainly be combated and made significantly easier to manage.

Once your debt has been adequately settled, you will be one step closer to removing this relentless and perpetual burden. With proper debt settlement, the load on your back will be lifted, and the possibility of living the good life will once again come to light.

If *debt* has been what has alienated you from living the life you want to live, then future debt is something you will want to avoid by all means necessary. The newly healthy cancer patient would never wish to have more cancer. The newly fit runner would never wish to return to a state of broken bones and an utter lack of fitness.

When the financial fat is hanging over your belt, it can be difficult to want to make a change. But with the right debt settlement plan, a significant portion of this fat can be removed, and you will feel lighter, freer, and more capable of achieving anything than ever before.

When asked how to reduce your actual level of fat, there will be few personal trainers who can promise you a solution that will take place overnight. As you will find in the financial industry, anyone who is offering a guaranteed solution is likely a part of a much larger scam. There are, however, many things you can do to immediately improve your financial health.

Throughout this book, this ongoing journey from a state of financial malaise to a state of financial fitness, we have described quite a few steps that you can take moving forward.

- *Recognize your debt for what is:* a means to an end, rather than something that is natural and is necessary.
- *Settle your debts* to the greatest extent you possibly can. Though your credit score will take a hit, settling your debts can relieve you of this perpetual burden and set you back on track to living the life you've always wanted.
- *Save before making major purchases:* If you do need to borrow (such as when getting a mortgage), building equity before borrowing will put you in a much more desirable situation.
- *Live within your means:* Though you may need a car and a home, choosing the more affordable option will lower your monthly payments and also end your debts sooner.
- *Find alternative sources of income:* As we saw with my grandparents in Boston, purchasing a duplex helped them achieve the dream of homeownership—without the unnecessary costs.
- *Realize that money is more important than your credit score:* Your credit score only really matters if you are trying to apply for more debt—something you should probably avoid to begin with.
- *Reject the "must have" ideology:* Creditors will always prefer people to borrow more and continue playing their game, rather than save and make responsible choices. It will be up to you to reject this destructive mind-set.

Even just a few years ago, the very notion of living a debt-free lifestyle was something that may have sounded completely foreign and unfamiliar.

While striving to achieve this objective will certainly be far from easy, just like losing ordinary fat can be difficult, it is certainly not impossible.

Debt does not need to be an essential part of who you are. Living the good life is certainly possible. With careful financial practices, a willingness to look for solutions, and the constant pursuit of financial freedom, the life you deserve is well within your reach. As we said earlier, every journey of a thousand miles begins with a single step.

There should be nothing stopping you from taking the next step forward.